This book
belongs to

Sunna

Bible
Praises *for*
PRESCHOOLERS

Written and Illustrated by
Kathy Arbuckle

BARBOUR
PUBLISHING, INC.
Uhrichsville, Ohio

© MCMXCVII by Barbour Publishing, Inc.

ISBN 1-57748-087-2

Scripture quotations are from the KING JAMES VERSION of the Bible.

Member of the
Evangelical Christian
Publishers Association

Published by Barbour Publishing, Inc.
            P.O. Box 719
            Uhrichsville, Ohio 44683
            http://www.barbourbooks.com

Printed in Hong Kong.

Thy Word is a lamp
unto my feet, and a
light unto my path.

Psalm 119:105

For Cousins

Michael Joseph,
Meghan Brooks
&
Erin Martha

Bible Praises for Preschoolers

But thou, O LORD, art a shield for me; my glory, and the lifter up of mine head.

Psalm 3:3

Long ago soldiers would carry shields with them into battle to protect themselves from the dangerous weapons of the enemy. God is like a shield for you. He loves you so much that He wants to protect you. His awesome power gives you strength and helps you hold your head high as He watches over you all day long. Tell Him today how much you love Him for keeping you safe.

My voice shalt thou hear in the morning, O LORD; in the morning will I direct my prayer unto thee, and will look up.

Psalm 5:3

Each morning the sun rises to wake you for a new day. The best way to begin every morning is to talk to God, pray to Him. If you start your morning looking up to God, He will guide you every minute of the rest of the day. We should use our time doing things that make God happy and telling Him how wonderful He is. So before you even get up out of bed, praise God and thank Him for His gift of a new day.

What can you praise God for today? 11

Bible Praises for Preschoolers

O LORD, our Lord, how excellent is thy name in all the earth!

Psalm 8:9

Is there anyone as good as God? Is there anyone as strong, as smart, as loving or patient or kind? No. God is the King of everything. He rules over the whole world and even the whole universe! We are happy to have such a wonderful God. We should tell others about how great He is and how much He loves all of us. Then we can all praise God together.

I will praise thee, O LORD, with my whole heart; I will show forth all thy marvelous works.

Psalm 9:1

Jesus said, "Love God with all of your heart." Look around you. Can you see all of the wonderful things God has made? He made all of the trees, flowers, animals, and even the mighty mountains. He has done so many amazing things for you and all of His family. But His most wonderful creation is you! So praise God with your whole heart, just as you love Him with your whole heart, because He has done such marvelous things.

Bible Praises for Preschoolers

I will sing unto the LORD, because he hath dealt bountifully with me.

Psalm 13:6

Did you know that everything you have is a gift from God? He gave you your family, good food to eat, clothes to wear, and a place to live. He even gives you extra things like the toys you play with or a cuddly pet to love. Your voice is also a gift. When you use it to sing songs of praise to God, it pleases Him. He deserves your praises of thanks and love.

I will bless the LORD, who hath given me counsel...

Psalm 16:7

Sometimes it is hard to know what to do. Every day there are decisions and choices for you to make. Let God guide you. He is like a map that shows a traveler which road to follow, or a ship's compass that guides a captain and his crew across the open sea to where they want to go. God even leads the ducks and geese on their way south for the winter. He will guide you, too. Just ask Him for help and praise Him for caring for you.

What can you praise God for today?   19

Bible Praises for Preschoolers

I will love thee, O LORD, my strength.

Psalm 18:1

Have you ever seen a strong man lifting heavy weights? He can pick up hundreds of pounds and hold them over his head. Some strong men win medals in contests because they are so very strong. God is much mightier than all of the most powerful men in the world put together! He is the one who gives you the strength to be the best person you can be. When you are weak He will be your strength. Let your love for God be strong, too.

Bible Praises for Preschoolers

The Lord liveth; and blessed be my rock; and let the God of my salvation be exalted.

Psalm 18:46

God is alive and is everywhere. He has always been alive and always will be. God is also powerful and is stronger than the strongest, tallest mountain. God gave us His son Jesus to save us from the bad things we do—our sins. Sin makes God very unhappy. The living God saved us so that we could live together with Him in heaven forever, after our life on earth is over. Praise God for giving us the special gift of eternal life with Him.

What can you praise God for today?

Bible Praises for Preschoolers

The heavens declare the glory of God; and the firmament showeth his handiwork.

Psalm 19:1

If you look up at the night sky, you see all of the twinkling stars and the bright, shining moon. When King David was a shepherd boy he would look up at the same stars. The very same moon we see would light up the pasture as he watched over the sheep. David thought about God every time he saw the beautiful stars and moon. Only God could make something that big and full of wonder. So each time you gaze at the night sky, think of God and praise Him.

I will declare thy name unto my brethren: in the midst of the congregation will I praise thee.

Psalm 22:22

There are many people who love God. If God is our Heavenly Father, then we are all brothers and sisters in God's big family. It is good for God's children to gather together to praise and worship Him. We can talk to each other about Him and share with others all about the wonderful things God has done for us. God delights in seeing His family together loving each other and loving Him with their praise.

What can you praise God for today? 27

Bible Praises for Preschoolers

The earth is the LORD'S, and the fullness thereof; the world, and they that dwell therein.

Psalm 24:1

God's special book, the Bible, tells of how God created the world and all of the different kinds of plants and animals. He formed the great mountains and filled the deep seas. He then made every type of plant to grow over all the earth. Then God, the Great Artist, caused all of the world's animals to come into being in all colors, shapes, and sizes. Even the best artist or smartest scientist in the world could never imagine all of the beautiful and amazing things God has created. He has made them all and they are all His.

The LORD is my strength and my shield; my heart trusted in him, and I am helped: therefore my heart greatly rejoiceth; and with my song will I praise him.

Psalm 28:7

Have you ever had a problem that was so big you did not know how to solve it? God knows everything and is more powerful than anyone or anything in the universe. Ask Him to help you solve your problem. He will help you. Just pray to Him and know that He will do what is best for you. And when your prayer is answered, praise Him for how good He is. Let your heart be happy, for God loves you so very much.

What can you praise God for today? 31

I will bless the Lord at all times: his praise shall continually be in my mouth.

Psalm 34:1

When is the best time to praise God? In the morning? At dinner time? When it is night? You should praise God all of the time! God never sleeps. All the day long He watches over you, protecting you, teaching you, loving you. Even when you are asleep at night He is right there covering you with His goodness and love, like a blanket. So, as you go through your day, remember to praise God every time you think of Him. After all, He never forgets about you.

What can you praise God for today?   33

Bible Praises for Preschoolers

O taste and see that the L ORD is good: blessed is the man that trusteth in him.

Psalm 34:8

Do you like ice cream, apple pie, or chocolate? All of these things taste so good. We like them so much that we come back for more! That is how God is. He is so good that you will always want to be near Him. Time with God is the most important part of your day. So talk to Him and give Him praise. You will be so happy knowing that your good and great Heavenly Father is taking perfect care of you.

Bible Praises for Preschoolers

Thy mercy, O LORD, is in the heavens; and thy faithfulness reacheth unto the clouds.

Psalm 36:5

Have you ever watched the clouds float way overhead in the sky? It's fun to find ones shaped like animals or castles or even people. Clouds are up very high in the air. God's faithfulness is as high as the clouds. He keeps every single promise He ever makes. He is also merciful, which means He doesn't always punish those who deserve to be punished. God's faithfulness and mercy reach all the way up to the clouds and even higher! Let your praise be heard up to the sky, too.

What can you praise God for today?

How excellent is thy lovingkindness, O God! Therefore, the children of men put their trust under the shadow of thy wings.

Psalm 36:7

When baby chickens hatch from eggs they are very small and need to be cared for. Their mother watches over them and teaches them how to find food so they can grow. Sometimes there is danger nearby and the mother hen gathers her babies under her wings to protect them. She will even shelter them beneath her wings at night to keep them warm and dry. God protects you like that. He keeps you safe under His wings of lovingkindness.

Bible Praises for Preschoolers

Many, O LORD my God, are thy
**wonderful works which thou hast
done, and thy thoughts which are
to usward...**

Psalm 40:5

Did you know God thinks about you?
King David said God has more thoughts
about you than there are grains of sand.
Just think about all the beaches, deserts,
and streambeds there are in the world
and how many tiny grains of sand there
must be. That is a lot of sand grains and
a lot of thoughts God has for you. You
are special to God, so special that He
wants to do wonderful things for you.
Let your thoughts today be filled with
praises for God.

What can you praise God for today?   41

Let all those that seek thee rejoice and be glad in thee: let such as love thy salvation say continually, The Lord be magnified.

Psalm 40:16

Many stories are about people looking for treasure. Why do they search for jewels and gold? Because the treasure is valuable and worth a lot. God's love for you is priceless. But God gives His love as a free gift to those who want to be close to Him. He should be the most important thing in your life. You will want to tell everyone about Him and show them His love. Just like a magnifying glass makes things easier to see, you can make God's love easier for others to see, too.

What can you praise God for today?

As the hart panteth after the water brooks, so panteth my soul after thee, O God.

Psalm 42:1

Deer are wild animals that live in the woods and meadows. Sometimes a deer can become very thirsty. He will search hard and walk a long way up and down hills and mountains until he finds a cool, clear stream to drink from. God is so good that you should be like that deer, only you are seeking after God, not water. If you are close to God, you can easily "drink" the love He has for you.

What can you praise God for today? 45

Hope thou in God: for I shall yet praise him, who is the health of my countenance, and my God.

Psalm 42:11b

To hope is to expect something good. The Bible tells us to put our hope in God. That means you should trust God to always take perfect care of you. He knows better than anyone else what is good for you. Your family, all of the things you have, the food you eat every day, even your health—all of these good things come from God. Praise Him for what He has done for you and also for the good things He will do for you in the future.

What can you praise God for today? 47

Bible Praises for Preschoolers

For God is the King of all the earth: sing ye praises with understanding.

Psalm 47:7

All the nations of the world have leaders or kings. Some of these leaders are very powerful and rule over large, wealthy countries of many people. But even if you took all of the leaders and their money and power and put them all together, they would not be anywhere close to being as great as God. God rules over the whole earth. He is so mighty that He reigns over the entire universe! Nothing happens without God knowing about it and letting it happen. Give great praise to the mighty Lord.

What can you praise God for today? 49

Whoso offereth praise glorifieth me...

Psalm 50:23

When you tell God how great He is you are praising Him. When you thank Him for all that He does for you and others you are praising Him, too. You can praise the Lord by talking to Him or praying, by singing songs to Him, even by drawing a picture for Him. He hears and sees all of your praises and He is pleased. Praise honors and glorifies God. It shows how important He is to you and how much you love Him.

What can you praise God for today? 51

Bible Praises for Preschoolers

In God I will praise his word, in God I have put my trust...

Psalm 56:4

God has given us His special book, the Bible, to teach us what is right. Even though the Bible was written so many, many years ago, it still teaches us today. God speaks to His people through the words He has written and shows us how to live and serve Him. The more you know about the Bible the more you know about God. You learn that you can trust Him to do what is best for you because He loves you so much. For that you should praise Him.

What can you praise God for today? 53

54   *Bible Praises for Preschoolers*

Make a joyful noise unto God, all ye lands...

Psalm 66:1

What noises sound happy to you?
Maybe people laughing, singing, clapping their hands and making music? All
over the world people know how to
make sounds of joy. When you think
about how special God is and about His
kindness and love, it makes you happy.
He gives you so many reasons to celebrate and rejoice. So sing and laugh.
Clap your hands and make music. Your
joyful praise will reach up to heaven and
please God's ears.

What can you praise God for today?

Bible Praises for Preschoolers

Blessed be the Lord, who daily loadeth us with benefits, even the God of our salvation.

Psalm 68:19

Think of the things God does for you every day. He makes the sun come up in the morning to brighten the world. He gives you love and takes care of you. God gives you good food to eat and clothes to wear. You may even have friends and toys to play with today. God gives you so much each day and often He gives you more than you need. He also gave His only Son Jesus to save you. Praise God for giving such precious gifts of love.

Let the heaven and earth praise him, the seas, and every thing that moveth therein.

Psalm 69:34

God is so amazing that all of His creation praises Him. All of the clouds, stars, the sun and moon, and the birds that fly in the sky praise God. If the rocks and mountains could speak, you would hear them praising the Creator, too. All of the animals that walk, run, hop, crawl, or slither on the ground give honor to the Lord. Even the waves on the sea leap with joy as they rejoice in praise. Join with all creation and praise the Lord!

What can you praise God for today?

Bible Praises for Preschoolers

But I will hope continually, and will yet praise thee more and more.

Psalm 71:14

Sometimes a problem can seem so big that you don't know how to solve it. No matter how big that problem is, it can never be bigger than God. You must remember to ask God for help when things look bad. You can always have hope because God is always with you to protect you and be your best friend. Best friends always care about each other.

What can you praise God for today?   61

For thou, Lord, art good, and ready to forgive; and plenteous in mercy unto all them that call upon thee.

Psalm 86:5

When you do a bad thing it makes God sad. It can also hurt the people around you. Even though your sin displeases God, He will forgive you and forget the sin if you tell Him you are very sorry and will try to never do that bad thing ever again. God is so good that He has lots of forgiveness to give to everyone who asks for it from their hearts. Praise our Holy God Who loves us enough to forgive us.

Bible Praises for Preschoolers

The LORD on high is mightier than the noise of many waters, yea, than the mighty waves of the sea.

Psalm 93:4

Have you ever been on a boat? Maybe you went out on a lake or river or even on the ocean. Did you see the waves? In a storm the waves on the water can grow to be very big because of the strong wind. They roar as they toss and crash, spraying water everywhere. There is a lot of power in the waves. God made all of the lakes, rivers, and seas and rules over them. There is no one mightier anywhere. His love for you is as strong as He is.

What can you praise God for today?   65

Enter into his gates with thanks-giving, and into his courts with praise: be thankful unto him, and bless his name.

Psalm 100:4

Do you celebrate Thanksgiving Day? Maybe you share a turkey dinner and enjoy some pumpkin pie for dessert with your family. Thanksgiving Day is a special day when we thank God for all He has given to us. But we should be thankful every day! After all, the Lord takes good care of us each and every day. Tell God "Thank you" in your praises and prayers every day of the year.

What can you praise God for today?   67

From the rising of the sun unto the going down of the same the Lord's name is to be praised.

Psalm 113:3

Does God do good things for only part of the day? Does He go away on vacation or take time off from His work? No. He is busy loving you and caring for you all of the time. You are so special and important to Him that He is always watching over you. What a good thing it is to be loved so much by God. All through the day, from sunrise to sunset, think about God and give Him praise.

I love the LORD, because he hath heard my voice and my supplications.

Psalm 116:1

Are you a good listener? Can you sit quietly while someone speaks to you? God is the greatest listener. He is able to hear everyone's prayers at the same time and answer those prayers when and how He knows it is best. God is never too busy to hear you. Even if you only have a little prayer about the smallest thing, He hears you. You can talk to God one hundred times a day and He will listen to every single word. He will always hear your praises, too.

What can you praise God for today? 71

This is the day which the LORD hath made; we will rejoice and be glad in it.

Psalm 118:24

God's book, the Bible, tells us that God made the earth, the sun and moon, the sky—everything. God also makes each day. Some days are sunny, some rainy or white with snow, but each one is a special gift to you from God. When you use each day to make God happy you will be happy, too. So praise God with happy songs and clapping hands for this is a joyful day!

74   *Bible Praises for Preschoolers*

How sweet are thy words unto my taste! yea, sweeter than honey to my mouth.

Psalm 119:103

Honey is very sweet, even sweeter than sugar. Our amazing God has taught bees how to make honey. Beekeepers are special farmers that raise bees for their honey so we can enjoy its delicious taste. God's book, the Bible, is like a beehive, but it is so full of goodness that it is better than honey. His Word teaches you how to be truly happy and tells how much He loves you. Nothing can be sweeter than that.

Bible Praises for Preschoolers

I was glad when they said unto me, Let us go into the house of the LORD.

Psalm 122:1

Church is where people come together as God's family. It is a special place where God is praised and worshipped in song and music. People learn more about God at church, too. At church you learn Bible stories, color pictures of Jesus and His friends, sing songs, and play games with other children. Can you think of a friend you might want to bring to church someday? It makes God glad to see His house filled with people who love Him and praise His name.

What can you praise God for today? 77

I will praise thee; for I am fearfully and wonderfully made: marvellous are thy works, and that my soul knoweth right well.

Psalm 139:14

God made everything in the universe. That means that He made you, too! He is the one who made your eyes brown or green or blue. He made your hair the color it is. He even knows how many hairs are on your head because He made each and every one of them! God put you together and made you the special person that you are. He looks at you with eyes that are filled with love for you. Praise Him with words that are filled with your love for Him.

What can you praise God for today?

Bible Praises for Preschoolers

I will sing a new song unto thee, O God: upon a psaltery and an instrument of ten strings will I sing praises unto thee.

Psalm 144:9

Do you know how to play a musical instrument? Making music is a way to praise God. You can sing along with the music using words that tell God how much He means to you. Music can be fancy, with grownups playing big instruments, or it can be simple, like you clapping your hands and singing with your voice. All music of praise is beautiful to God's ears.

Bible Praises for Preschoolers

One generation shall praise thy works to another, and shall declare thy mighty acts.

Psalm 145:4

Your mommy and daddy love God and they love you. They want you to know all about God so you will love Him, too. That is why they teach you about the Bible and tell you the stories that are written in God's Holy Book. Maybe your Grandma and Grandpa also share with you about the greatness of God. Grownups teach the children so the family will all love and praise the Lord together.

What can you praise God for today?

84   *Bible Praises for Preschoolers*

Praise ye the LORD: for it is good to sing praises unto our God; for it is pleasant; and praise is comely.

Psalm 147:1

Do you feel good about yourself when someone tells you what a good job you did on something? Maybe you made your bed neatly or cleaned up your toys or brushed your teeth all by yourself. God does so many wonderful things for you. He always does an extra-good job on His work. He deserves extra-special praises for all that He does. He loves to receive your words and songs of praise. They are lovely to Him.

Great is our Lord, and of great power: his understanding is infinite.

Psalm 147:5

If all of the smartest people in the whole world met in one place and put all their knowledge together, that knowledge would only be a tiny part of what God knows. He knows everything there is to know. His power is as great as His wisdom. He makes the earth turn in space and the lightning flash from the sky. His strong arms protect you as He guides you with His wisdom. No one is greater than Almighty God.

Bible Praises for Preschoolers

Sing unto the LORD with thanksgiving; sing praise upon the harp unto our God: Who covereth the heaven with clouds, who prepareth rain for the earth, who maketh grass to grow upon the mountains.

Psalm 147:7,8

Do you like to watch the rain come down? God causes the clouds to form in the sky like a blanket over the earth. Then the rain begins to fall when He tells it to. The falling rain nourishes the plants and makes them grow. All of the flowers, grass, bushes, and trees need water to grow, so God showers them with rain just like He showers you with His love.

What can you praise God for today?   89

Praise ye him, all his angels...

Psalm 148:2

Did you know that the angels praise God? They know all about God's greatness. He is holy, kind, strong, and wise. He is patient, forgiving, good, and full of love for you and all His family. The angels know these things and they give God praise all day and all night. You can be like the angels by praising God, too.

What can you praise God for today?

Bible Praises for Preschoolers

Kings of the earth, and all people;
princes, and all judges of the earth:
Both young men, and maidens; old
men, and children: Let them praise
the name of the Lord...

Psalm 148:11-13

God is Lord over all the people of the
earth. It does not matter if you are very
rich or poor, a powerful leader or someone's servant. God loves you and will
hear you when you praise Him. If you
are a boy or a girl, young or old, big or
small, weak or strong there is no differ-
ence to God. You are important to Him.
Join with all of God's children everywhere and praise His name.

What can you praise God for today?   93

Every day will I bless thee; and I will praise thy name for ever and ever.

Psalm 145:2

God does not have a birthday. He has always been and will always be. He never stops caring for you and loving you, not even for one second. At night when you are asleep God is right there being your loving protector. Every day is the right day to praise God. And because you believe in Jesus you will be able to praise God forever in heaven, too.

What can you praise God for today? 95

Let every thing that hath breath
praise the LORD. Praise ye the LORD.

Psalm 150:6